55 Coincidences

Was that God Knocking?

Ed Mikulski

FIFTY-FIVE COINCIDENCES:
WAS THAT GOD KNOCKING?

TABLE OF CONTENTS

INTRODUCTION

I was raised in a Catholic family in a mostly Lithuanian-American section of Scranton, Pennsylvania. By Catholic standards my life has not been a holy one, and I have not held true to the standards of the Catholic Church. Let us just say that my father and a number of others would say that I have just not measured up. My father particularly has said as much.

Yet I do believe that God has found me. I do not know why this has happened.   Certainly there are many more faithful, obedient, worthy, and intelligent people. Yet I have had, to my mind, an incredible number of "coincidences" in my life, enough to prove to me at least, that there is a God somewhere out there who knows me, and who has intervened heavily in the events of my life.

I would like to think of this onslaught of "coincidences" as proof to me that an active supernatural being exists. My faith says to me that this supernatural being is God. Others with intransigent religious or philosophical beliefs may argue that my set of "coincidences" is evidence of something other than a loving God, or just simply nothing at all.

I challenge them with my own firm belief, evident in the stories that I will relate, in overwhelming evidence not only of a supernatural force, but evidence of a supernatural force that is very loving. As all this "coincidence" happened to me, I felt shocked as the possibility that these events happened just by chance became more and more remote, actually unbelievable. The weight of these events hit me very hard, and so repeatedly.

My hope is that my story will be believed, and that it will be a source of firm faith in God for some of those who read it. Rather than hoping that my story is the only one like this, I would love to find out that others will report that something like this has happened to them too. I would be very willing to take any test on the veracity of these events. Very many of these events are perfectly traceable.

I have read recently that the temperature of much of "outer space" is something like minus-455 degrees Fahrenheit, and that the farthest known galaxy from us is 13.1 billion light years away. Yet people still love their lives on earth and what is in them. They root for their favorite team, think they might magically hit the lottery, and believe that their opinions and their loved ones are somehow best in this vast, mostly cold universe. There seems to be much room here for beauty, love, and feeling special.

Is love not more important than the religious/philosophical belief system you or I were born into, in whichever country we were born? I personally believe that the almighty force loves you, and he loves me.

Just as well, I seem to have heard that very many people have had at least a few experiences similar to the ones I am about to describe in this writing. Please read on, and consider your own experiences too.

CHAPTER 1
Coincidences from 1999 to 2004

CHAPTER 1
Coincidences from 1999 to 2002

Personal coincidences will be listed by number, but not exactly in the order that they happened. Basically, the events are listed in Column A, with further explanation listed in Column B.

A

1. I was hired from Cincinnati as a social worker on the 85-person staff at Daytona V.A. Clinic, start date May 8, 2001..

B

My next-door neighbor in Cincinnati, Dan, was offered a transfer to the Daytona V.A. Clinic, same start date of May 8, 2001. Neither of us knew the other had applied. With over 200,000V.A. employees at the time, and our two different job titles, this was a very long shot. What were the odds?

2. On September 14, 2001, a film on P. O. W.'s I had produced and mostly written opened at Cincinnati V.A> Hospital. Reportedly "not a dry eye" in the house. I could not attend from Florida due to flight cancellations, and my booking error.

There are only 612 P.O.W.'s who returned from Vietnam. My mother-in-law sold her house in 2001 to move in with my wife and me. The purchaser of the house was the child of one of the 612 and one who was very well known to Senator McCain and others of the P.O.W.'s. A coincidence, especially with the film's timing. Also, Russ, the only Vietnam-era P.O.W. who appeared in our film, was shot down the very day before Senator McCain was, on October 27, 1967. Both released March, 1973. McCain was sent copy of the film to share.

3. A veteran at Daytona V.A. Clinic asked if I could give him rides every other week for 6 weeks to St. Augustine for him to get dentures.

I was already scheduled for rare meetings in St. Augustine every other Friday to prepare for a veterans' "stand down." When the veteran with the dentures called in a year to ask for a ride for his follow-up visit "Ha, ha, ha" he said, I already had another rare meeting scheduled there, and provided the ride. 52 miles away and unknown why his dental appointments were this far. In 5 1/2 years at Daytona Clinic, I only had two stand downs in St. Augustine, so go figure the odds.

4. My wife and I were two of hundreds of people who attended a volunteer appreciation luncheon in Daytona. News anchor Wendy Chioji was the MC. The veteran at our table was announced as Volunteer of the Year. He introduced us to his wife, Florence and his cousin Gretchen, who was visiting from Connecticut.

My wife's name is Gretchen, my mother-in-law living with us 2001 - 2004 was Florence. To add to that, I was one of 9 of the 100+ agency reps chosen to receive a free "hot lap" at Daytona Speedway as a door prize. Long shot that the man at our table chosen from hundreds to receive his award that year. Gretchen/Florence coincidence seemed to be rare also.

5. The phone number at the new V.A. Clinic that opened in 2001 is 323-7500

My mother-in-law went into assisted living in 2002. Her new phone number was 343-7500.

6. My license number moving to Daytona in May, 2001, was D30 FMA.

My wife's friend in Daytona, our real estate agent, had license D10 FMA. The agent, Barbara S., noticed.

7. I "witnessed" about my belief in a loving higher power to my friend at work in Cincinnati 1998/1999.

In 1999, my friend reported to me on a scary accident he had while driving his teenage daughter on I-75. He reported his van was severely damaged as a truck tire from the opposite direction flew through their front window between their bucket seats. The van as in very bad shape, but neither person was inured.

8. In September, 2002, I discussed with a friend the coincidences listed above, as well as dozens of others t follow. Her son, whom I worked with in a very small youth group at church, was named Kyle. There was a hurricane that year named Kyle as well and my friend and I discussed how it might be coincidental that the hurricane turned out to be special.

It seemed coincidental timing that I had to take the beltway all the way around the metro area due to the perfect timing of the ramp closure. Since that 1999 spill, Dawn is routinely used to clean up grease spills.

10. In church in 2000, I made a rare request for prayer for a friend, Dave D…. Who was going through a tough time. But I misspoke his name as "say a prayer for Don D…"

In a few months, I had a successful job interview for a spot in Florida. The head of the hiring committee turned out to have the name Don D…(same last name). On consecutive days I was offered difficult-to-get jobs in Daytona, then Florida west coast the next. My wife knew Daytona was my first choice, not hers, and she said "Ed, you take Daytona."" A wonderful statement. Daytona has been a wonderful place for both of us also.

10. In church in 2000, I made a rare request for prayer for a friend, Dave D…. Who was going through a tough time. But I misspoke his name as "say a prayer for Don D…"

In a few months, I had a successful job interview for a spot in Florida. The head of the hiring committee turned out to have the name Don D…(same last name). On consecutive days I was offered difficult-to-get jobs in Daytona, then Florida west coast the next. My wife knew Daytona was my first choice, not hers, and she said "Ed, you take Daytona."" A wonderful statement. Daytona has been a wonderful place for both of us also.

11. In late March 1999, a supervisor piles a huge workload in a worker in a group where I was a first-line supervisor.

Now a friend of mine had told me that I would have good luck if and when people would try to "get me". Well, on what I remember t be March 18th, I snowed well over a foo and travel conditions changed "huge workload" into "almost nothing to do" for my worker in this isolated incident. Possible disaster that was planned for March 18ᵗʰ became a joke. I'm going to guess that God doesn't really want to "get even" with meanness in any way, just likes a good chuckle too. Shows a lot of love, "to even me." And to my co-worker.

12. I "flipped out" in December, 2002 due to personal factors and the realization of all this coincidence. I took sick leave for over 2 months, which stopped me at 1,999.75 hours of sick leave, shot of my lifetime goal of 2,000. I do have the yellowed pay stub still.

Ironically, another lifetime goal was reached that day while going home sick. After years of living in Pa., Florida, and other bear country states, I finally saw my First Bear, a black bear, while driving from Gainesville to Daytona through the Ocala National Forest. My co-worker Betty corroborates this. It was a cute bear, about 4 feet tall, standing by the side of the road and hitchhiking. Even in dire times, I think God has a nice and gentle was of showing us love.

And oh, by the way, the day I wrote the introduction to this book, in late November, 2015, three couples sat in a lounge listening to a musical performance by our friend. The server noticed that two of the bills came up exactly $48.93, though greatly different items had been ordered. He thought it was worth mentioning and the date that this happened also seemed a coincidence to me. Many numbers coincidences are described later in this work.

CHAPTER 2

Family and Friends' Coincidences

CHAPTER 2

Family and Friends' Coincidences

1. In 1990, my father told me that my brother and I were big and tall like the peach tree in his back yard and that we were also, like that peach tree, "without fruit, worthless." When that tree would have any peaches at all, they would be hard and skinny and sappy.

On September 5, 1995, my brother died, during peach harvest season. My mother insisted that I take some peaches back to Cincinnati. So many hot tears were shed. Only when I got to Cincinnati from Scranton, did I taste and find the ten or so peaches I had picked were just firm and delicious, as a gift from my father above. Also, within maybe one hour of my return on that Sunday, red gerbera daisies from co-workers arrived at our house. I was told later that no one knew that red gerbera daisies were my favorites. But it happened that way.

2. There were 3 hurricanes in 2004 that caused damage in Daytona, as well as a 4th, Hurricane Ivan, that struck elsewhere in Florida, then went up the eastern seaboard. My father and mother-in-law died on consecutive Sundays in 2004.

Hurricane Ivan washed out the road to the Scranton, Pa. nursing home where my father died on 9-18-04. My mother-in-law died on 9-25-04 as Hurricane Jeanne hit Daytona. I was the last family member to see both - saw my father last on 9-17 due to a rare road washout on 9-18. Ivan a rare weather event in Pennsylvania.

3. My brother, father, mother-in-law and father-in-law all died during the month of September. My mother later had "last rites" one September, but did not pass away till that November

My mother was born 1-6-21, dies 11-21-06. My brother died 9-5-95. My father died the day before his birthday (87th) and my maternal grandmother died the day before her birthday (65th)

4. On August 4, 2007, my stepson went to Yankee Stadium from North Carolina for a baseball game as his wife's 40th birthday present to him. In the first inning, he got a cell phone call from his sister in Pennsylvania wishing him a happy birthday. They speak maybe once a year.

During the call, Alex Rodriguez hit a home rum for his 500th career homer, making him the youngest ever to reach that number. Jim held the phone up for his sister to hear the great cheering. Coincidentally that night Barry Binds hit his 755th career homer, tying Hank Aaron for the all-tie most home runs. That same day in Jim's town of Winston-Salem was also the funeral of a young Skip Prosser, a successful basketball coach first in Cincinnati (Xavier) then in Jim's Winston-Salem (Wake Forest). Sister is Jan.

5. Jan graduated from university in Carolina in December, 1993 with a B. A. in English. Despite the mid-year graduation date, we enjoyed the commencement address of Bishop Desmond Tutu.

When she graduated with a second degree in English from engineering school, 2001, speaker as Bill Nye, the science guy. It is ironic that she would choose this school on a firm recommendation from one of her professors to study English, as her two cousins had also attended there, but studied Engineering. Jan and my cousin Richard also both attended Duke, as my friend Don D...from Chapter 1 had strong ties there too. Jan's primarily-engineering school was over 800 miles from her home.

6. I had a reunion lunch on 6/27/15 with a mother and her two children whom I had not met with in the 11 years since they were in my youth group. Also, I had advised the mother about her service-connected disability claim 11 years or more ago.

The next day, on 6/28/15, the woman finally got a call after 11 years of waiting that she will have a hearing on her service-connected claim I 3 weeks. By 7/1/15, there were two clips in our News-Journal paper about Kevin Nash a movie star and former pro wrestler we gleefully met during a youth group outing to a local church festival 11 years prior. Nash is 6' 10", with a lot of presence.

7. As further evidence of continuing "luck," in March, 2015 I backed my car up in our condo parking lot and backed into a yellow pole. But, I missed breaking my tail light by the tiniest margin, such as there is still yellow paint along the red tail light.

Also, once my ex-wife had a car accident in the evening, then called me next morning in tears about the car accident. Turned out she called about an accident with the other car—two accidents in less than 24 hours. Not so lucky.

8. My brother-in-law and sister-in-law have birthdays on January 3rd and 6th, my step granddaughter was born February 19th, my step-son and wife married January 10th.

On my side, cousin Jimmie born January 3rd, my mother born January 6th, my first wife February 19th, my brother January 10th.

9. My mother's social security number had 5 of the same numbers in a row. I still have the card in my possession.

The other four numbers in her SS# were two more pairs, a rare "hand." Another close person had a SS# with "4 of a kind" twice in the nine numbers.

Chapter 3

Weather and Travel Longshots

Chapter 3

Whether and Travel Longshots

1. On December 3, 2010, we began a 2-week trip to Egypt, returning home 12/17/2017 with an overnight near JFK in New York. We left New York right before a large snowstorm and also just missed fatal crash of Aswan to Abu Simbel bus that happened on 12/26/2010

In January 25, 2011, all the trouble with Mubarak and Egypt erupted and Egypt has not been the same since. In addition, a woman sat next to our group on the flight from New York to Atlanta; she was from Cairo and her baby had a serious hearing impairment, as did the woman of the couple that accompanied us to Egypt.

2. I was stranded overnight on a train in Cresco, Pa in 1954 for Hurricane Hazel, also evacuated from St. Pete area home in 1985 for Hurricane Elena and in 2004 for 3 hurricanes - Charlie, Frances and Jeanne.

I was in southern California for the L.A. earthquake of 1971, was in Boston for the two 1978 snowstorms. Evacuated from Bayonne, N. J. for major oil refinery fire in 1956 and was in Bayonne on Newark Bay the day a train fell into the bay, killing N. Y. Yankee George Stirnweiss and others, September 1958. Saw the Stirnweiss headline in the Bayonne Times. We were in Bayonne visiting my mon's relatives; I was 9 then.

3. I was in Omaha for the huge May 1974 tornado, the third costliest tornado of all time.

From the 10th floor of the hospital where I worked on 42nd Street, I watched the huge funnel turn from northeastward to north, right up 72nd street. From this unique vantage point on a hill west of downtown, I could see at least 5 smaller funnels as well and the debris looked like flocks of flying birds.

4. We flew from Tampa to Cincinnati the day of the "Storm of the Century," March 12, 1983. Most flights cancelled or delayed. Encountered closed bridges and wife an extra hour at car rental due to computers going down. I prayed out loud on way to airport.

Got to departure gate 2 hours late, at which time I heard final boarded call. Yet, plane still not fully boarded until another half-hour later when wife arrived from car rental area. In Cincinnati, there were just 6 lucky inches of wet snow, while Columbus to the north and Lexington to the south both got over 2 feet. Columbus 107 miles from Cincinnati, Lexington 82 miles from Cincinnati.

5. Our first cruise was May 8, 2002 on Star Princess to Alaska.

Also on ship were 6 people form our former church in Cincinnati - organist head deacon, etc. I don't think we "measured up" at that church, so not much was said. But my wife had much fun playing mah jongg with people on board from China, despite no one able to speak same language, except a little girl who translated.

6. In January, 2006, we signed up for a May transatlantic cruise on the Norwegian Jewel.

In early February, 2006 then, that ship was featured on a 5-morning ABC special with Diane Sawyer. Fun to watch all week.

7. In June 0f 1985, a large line of severe weather including tornadoes broke out over New York state, Maryland, etc. I had flown back unannounced to Dover, Delaware and found wife and child not home. I had no key.

I spent the night lying on steps of our storm cellar, as large hail and rain beat down on the cellar door. Concrete steps & loud rattling.

Chapter 4

Sports Coincidences

Chapter 4

Sports Coincidences

1. In 2003, I attended the Funai Golf Classic practice round at Disney. We followed Vijay Singh and Bob Burns. Singh asked Burns if he had played the tournament the previous year.

In our little group of maybe 10 to 15 people closely following this pair, Burns replied that he had played in 2002 and had won! Ironically, Singh later that week won the 2003 Funai.

2. At my 25th high school reunion weekend, our Scranton Prep football team beat Tunkhannock 21 - 20 via a 10-yard pass as time expired, plus the extra point, in 1991.

3. Also in 1991, I attended only one basketball game the entire year and the high school girls team had their only win of the year that night on a free throw made after time had expired to 00 second.

I have almost never otherwise attended any high school athletic events in the past 49 years. So, both 1991 events being won after time expired - neat.

4. At my only other high school reunion attended, the 40th, the two people in the parking lot after our separate rounds of golf were me and another person and we had the only Florida license tags.

The other person was Sandy Koufax whom I had seen pitch when I was a youth. The "greatest ever" Koufax that day won 17 - 2 on a 3-hitter and he himself hit a double at Shea Stadium. Also for the L. A. Dodgers, Tommy Davis was 5-for-5 Jim Lefebvre and Al Ferrara each hit 2 homers.

5. I attended Marquette University beginning in the 1966-'67 school year. That was the third year of legendary coach Al McGuire. His two previous years, the team was 8-18 and 14-12.

In march, 1967 Marquette went 21-9 and runner up in the NIT tournament. My 3 years there were at the beginning of a great stretch of success, culminating in 1977, winning the NCAA national championship.

6. I was in the stands when the NCAA's first field goal ever of 60 yards was kicked, at the University of Arkansas.

The ball landed in the tuba section of the band, which was lined up. The Sports illustrated article said "Oompa." Bill McClard was the kicker and the SMU kicker also made a wind blown 50-yarder. Not too many people were at this event and also the 1978 Boston snowstorms. Just sayin'.

7a. Tiger Woods on this tournament, which helped him separate himself as the #1 player in golf, 1999.

I have followed pairs or groups at only 6 PGA practice rounds in addition to the Burns/Singh round and enjoyed many moments. One was my wife referring to a young Hunter Mahan as "Cowboy" for his looks and long blond hair and following winners Choi in 2011 and Kuchar (with Woodland in 2012 , hitting endless practice chips to a green on the back 9). Mahan really is a "cowboy," having played at Oklahoma State. All Players Championship in Vedra Beach.

8. In 2007, I purchased a ticket for a bucket of golf balls to hit at a driving range in Daytona.

The number on the ticket was 43444444.

9. Our Norwegian Jewel transatlantic cruise got to Rome late May, 2006. Made friends with our tour driver in Rome and E-Mailed after return home.

Shared his joy as Italy won the World Cup, June to July 2006. Celebration was at Circus Maximus. Famous head butt incident in final game.

10. In 1998, my wife and I saw the Atlanta Braves beat Cincinnati 7 - 6 on a 2-run homer by David Justice in the 9th. This led to the Braves winning the pennant over the perennial winning L. A. Dodger.

Joe Oliver even had a grand-slam for Cincinnati. But many Cincinnati fans cheered Justice's important home run because of ill feelings for the Dodgers. But from here on for about a decade, the Braves took over as the perennial championship winners.

11. In 1993, we saw the Toronto Blue Jays play the Philadelphia Phillies in a spring training game.

These two teams later played each other in the October, 1993 World Series. Phillies' Mitch Williams was entertaining in the bullpen.

12. I tried to be catcher on my high school baseball team.

The other catcher trying out was famous NBA basketball coach P. J. Carlesimo. I was only qualified to be a catcher, so I became the catcher, while he, one of our best hitters, was shortstop.

13. I believe it was the televised 2005 Honda Golf Classic that a player hit a ball that bounced in the air off jagged rocks a total of about 7 times.

I did not experience this event in person, just on T. V., so I am not sure of the date. But it was absolutely phenomenal to watch. Four or five times would even have been "unreal".

Chapter 5

A Few Other Coincidences

Chapter 5

A Few Other Coincidences

1. When I was 15, my mother took me to a lake near Scranton so I could fish. I had to pass about 40 water snakes on a spillway, both going to and returning from my "spot". At the end of the day, I hitch-hiked my way back to town riding on a truck that happened to be delivering a mattress to the house next door to ours.

2. When I was a teenager, I saw the Muppets on T.V. for the first time on the Ed Sullivan show. Really liked Kermit the Frog. At a church block party maybe a year later, there were tickets to purchase for 20 possible prizes, with the only winners being those that ended with "00" such as "100", "200", up to "2000." The prize for 1300 was to be a very cute green-with-yellow stuffed frog. I won him with just a dollar or two paid. He was in our house on back of the couch for years - Kermit.

3. In August, 1967, I had a definite dream of a silvery– gray casket. I searched the newspaper and next morning saw an obituary of Mr. Henry Kaiser, the aluminum industry magnate. My only such dream, but caught my attention.

4. The pastor of the church I led youth group with had an M. S. W. degree, as does Senator Mikulski, as do I. Though I left the church pastored by the man with the M. S. W. degree in 2002, the T. V. show "Numb3rs" was started in 2005.

A main character on that show had some name pronunciation as that pastor's. First and last name.

6. I lives in Allentown in 1982 when Billy Joel recorded the song "Allentown."

A little chuckle that Billy Joel declined city of Allentown's request to share hi profits on the song.

7. I believe I passed through Chicago when Richard Speck committed his atrocities. Also in New York weekend of Gorbachev visit to 1988 and saw Soviet flag outside Plaza Hotel. Toured submarine USS Wyoming in Georgia 11/13/14 just before story broke 12/04/14 about sailors taking pictures of females.

Pre-admission trip to Marquette University on train from Scranton to Milwaukee only reason I would note date in July, 1966 of the Speck story.

8. In 2006, my mother and wife and two strangers were waiting in line to check out in a grocery store in north Scranton I had two pennies which I reached in my pocket for.

I have never done anything like this before or since, but I repeated words to the effect of "I'd like to put ,u two cents in, I'd like to spend these pennies, etc." The bill came to $21.02, so one of the three asked "How'd you do that?" I said something like, "Well, either everything's magic, or nothing's magic."

9. In December, 2012 to January, 2013, my wife and I went on a cruise to South America, ending with a few days in Buenos Aires. In March, 2013, the new Pope was elected.

Showing faith in purposeful coincidences in my life, I read and considered an article with a list of about 25 serious candidates to be the new Pope. I wrote down the name "Bergoglio" on a slip of paper because he is from Buenos Aires. This became Pope Francis I. One out of 25 not really a long shot, but it does show my belief.

10. In 1991 a friend kept trying to persuade me to become a believer. He kept saying that if I did not act, "the train of my chances to do so would pull out of the station," or words to that effect. I was 43 then.

Trying to look to the Bible for help in making this decision, I opened the book randomly and my eyes went right to the verse about Ephraim in Hosea: "gray hairs are here and there upon him, yet he knoweth not." If you think it's easy to land upon this verse, go ahead and try it right now.

11. So at about 2 A. M. on the morning of December 31, 1991, I go out of bed and prayed a prayer to accept God into my life and heart.

Back in bed, it was not three seconds before I heard a train horn sounding in the background. And it is just now that I am writing this that I am connecting the fact that I was born at the hour of 2 A. M.

Chapter 6

Some Coincidences for Others

Chapter 6

Some Coincidences for Others

Interestingly, it seems to me that not many provable works have been written on the subject of coincidences. But I would like to add a few other odd facts, not from my life, but "out there" that seem to point to the thought that some events are in line with a supernatural purpose, rather than just a random collection of facts.

1. The 1989 World Series between bay area teams, Oakland and San Francisco. Four minutes after the first game of the series to be played in San Francisco (Game 3 of the series) came on the air, the big earthquake hit.

The timing of the long-expected earthquake was quite a long shot, with cameras in place and right to the moment in time.

2. The Big Dipper and the Little Dipper are the only truly distinc-tively shaped objects in the sky. The are seen in pretty perfect align-ment from the earth's perspective. They might look like nothing from another angle.

The fact that these two look like man-made objects, both with 4 stars in the dippers and 3 in the handles is amazing. These sole distinctively shaped objects look exactly similar. Why is that? The fact that the important north star is part of the Little Dipper seems another compounded long shot. Why Looking So Man-Made?

3. With much smaller odds, Pope John Paul II believed it was a mira-cle that he was shot on the very day (May 13th) and hour that the

I believe his one in 8,760 chance (365 x 24) of being shot at the date and time of the Fatima anni-versary is quite a long shot. That purported appearance at Fatima happened. He felt it was miraculous that he did not die from the gunshot.

late Pope, though Polish by birth, is ethnically half-Lithuanian. I am fully Lithuanian-American. We share something there, coincidentally?

Chapter 7

Discussion and Challenge

Chapter 7

Discussion and Challenge

Most of the events that were coincidental and totally "blew my mind" happened in the very few years from 1999 until my "aha" moment in December, 2002. Ever since that time, I have intended to write about the events.

I did write vignettes about some of the things that happened way back then, and have since 2002 added many more stories. But I had never before this time put it all together. At times it has felt like writer's block, and my inaction created in me a feeling of guilt for not acting on a gift that was given to me. But there has also been a feeling of confidence in this not-too-confident person that one day it would get done, at the right time.

At times I have "shared" about my stories, and did not get any positive response. My doctor wanted to "up" my medication, and challenged me, asking whether I had any coincidences to tell about related to 9/11. I kept my mouth shut.

This was so, even though the only film I had ever written/produced "opened" to a very patriotic audience of hundreds of veterans, including ex-POW's, on 9/14/01. I could not attend because of the many flight cancellations due to the 9/11 events. And I also did not tell him about my other extremely strong long shots involving at least one or two other ex-POW's. Our film narrator was Elaine Camerota, mother of Alisyn. For reference, the website for Vietnam P.O.W.'s is "Three's In," with the list of P.O.W's under "Other Interesting Facts...."

I have mentioned my unlikely-to-be-randomly-occurring experiences to family members before, with little in the way of positive response or belief. I guess some would like my doctor to up my medication as well.

In about the year 2012, I joined a poetry group in east central Florida. This got me involved in writing poems, averaging about one per month. For the past three years, I have become better at writing, and this has been what was possibly needed for me to finish this work. The poetry group came along at a very good time.

Finally, in August, 2015, I handed a nearly completed manuscript of this work to my friend who leads the poetry group, and he told me in September 2015 that he felt all these events happened by chance, however remote. Oh well, I knew in advance that my friend was not really a believer anyway. Maybe he will change, but he is wonderful, and I guess he doesn't need to.

But, maybe coincidentally, I learned through my poetry connections of a local workshop on the subject of getting a manuscript published, which was held in October, 2015. I said to myself that maybe I would attend and get my work published if I can finish it, or maybe just even get a book of my poems published.

Was I ever rewarded by attending that workshop! I had of course heard that finding a publisher for a work is not easy. Maybe even telling a story like mine to some groups of people is going to lead to laughter as well. But in this case, as they say in France, "Au contraire!"

The workshop I went to was peopled by good and enthusiastic folks, who were also enthusiastic about being believers. Oh yes, I had to travel a whole 3.0 miles to get to the workshop on that evening! But all in all, I think that is ...excellent timing and place.

I would like very much for a statistician to go through all the events described in this work and give an idea as to what the odds are that the entire list of what has happened to me in one lifetime can be explained by chance. A good exercise even for the reader would be to re-read some of the events, and then guess the odds of #4, $6, and #7 in Chapter Two all happening to the same person, as well as the first six or so of Chapter One. These would be just 10 of the over 50 coincidences describe in this book.

And there have been other events. For example, on January 3, 2011, my long-lost and re-found cousin Johnny died in Cochise County, Arizona just before the Giffords shooting incident in a Tucson suburb on January

8, 2011, followed by my helping interview our current pastor from Tucson about that same month, with his start date in Florida March, 2011 The husband of one of my wife's two best friends in Daytona is also from Tucson, a long way away from here. Is it overdoing it to add that the co-host of our co-favorite T.V. show (Dancing with the Stars) in 2011 was Brooke Burke, from Tucson?

My wife's friend and her husband from Tucson live at an address beginning with 925, my address begins with 925, and when I was checking mileage from my address to the address of the publishing workshop mentioned just above, I discovered that it is 925 as well. So, the Tucson/925 streak is a long one. And, there are others that I have not listed here.

Yet to estimate the odds of all this happening, it is really not important which person this happened to, just that it happened, in sequence, to one person. Most just seemed to "happen," not as the result of any planning. And, if special powers exist out there, do we not all share in them?

A good number of people I have run into have expressed that they have similar experiences in their lives, though probably not so many! These people tend to be believers in an almighty force. I think that many, but not all, also feel that this is a force that demonstrates not only unimaginable breadth and depth, but also shows that on earth love and sometimes infinitesimally small items of beauty are also important.

Well, if it seems that serendipity has happened in your life, you know that I hope this is actual truth for you as well. The fact that so much of this has happened in my life, I hope is an encouragement to you about the definite existence of an almighty force, and of its love for "even us."

On the other hand, I would challenge those who do not believe in an almighty force to reconsider. What are the odds of the serendipity of our beautiful earth just emerging on its own and rotating perfectly in this huge and barren universe?

If you cannot even figure the possibility of the perfect symmetry of "pi" and everything else, maybe there is someone or something which can and has already done it.

So is all the above mathematical proof of something?? I would like to say, like Sky King in the T.V. action-adventure series of my youth: "Penny, this case is closed." Yet, faith is a funny thing, and preconceived notions are what they are. So it is up to each person to work out their beliefs.

ADDITIONAL NOTES

ADDITIONAL NOTES

1. More early January: I retired from the V.A. on January 3, 2006, and then finally found Mental Health America job/volunteer job that I love on January 3, 2011 (there's January, 2011 again too). This was after having searched many activities to make my retirement fulfilling. The day I signed with the Navy, my service computation date, was January 6, 1970. How busy early January has been. My wife and I were married on January 9, 1992. My birthday is a little off – December 27.

2. The very weekend before I retired from the V.A. (1/3/06 as above), I went to see the Rockettes in Orlando, about 90 miles away. In a building across the street from the performance, I ran into another "Don" while entering men's room, a man who worked very closely with me on getting veterans a V.A. pension. He had also been in Omaha metro area during the 1974 tornado, and I had recently given him and his wife the yellowed newspaper article on the tornado that my mom had saved for me.

3. Our late real estate agent, Barbara S., just became locally famous for donating a very large sum of money to renovate a local playhouse.

4. P.J. Carlesimo's father Pete was executive director of the N.I.T basketball tournament from 1978 to 1988, and was responsible for the ruling called the "Al McGuire Rule," referring to the Marquette basketball coach.

5. The view I had of the 1974 Omaha tornado was exceptional in that the building I worked at was situated west of downtown Omaha high up on 42nd Street, not only nearer the tornado, but also because *most* tall buildings in Omaha are east of the big hill around 30th Street and nearer the level of the river. I was in the Naval Reserves at the time, and we helped in the cleanup on our drill weekend.

6. We also went to see Rory McIlroy the week after his famous first win at Quail Hollow, but it was another member of his foursome, the unknown Graeme McDowell, who had his first win the following month at the U.S. Open, which is concluded every year on Father's Day Sunday.

7. Koufax's plate was St. Lucie County, mine was Volusia County. He wore a very nice white and blue striped golf shirt the day I saw him.

8. I have a copy of the April, 2006 sports section of the Atlanta Journal-Constitution. It has a picture of Masters Tournament golfer Stuart Ap-

pleby, but refers to him as "Robert Allenby," a different golfer, also from Australia. You don't see that kind of thing very often. I contend that most of the events that happened to me seem much more like something that just fell on me out of the clear blue. Maybe, in a very few cases like this, not so much that way.

9.   My mom's close friend in assisted living was a man named Edgar, who had played in the NFL, though my mom had never before heard of him. He played in the same backfield as Marion Motley and Otto Graham, shortly before Jim Brown joined the Cleveland Browns. I myself felt honored to meet "Special Delivery" Jones.

10.   Our local dentists had the same first names as my wife's son and his father. It was striking seeing that dentists' sign almost every day for years.

11.   Larry Holmes won the heavyweight boxing championship from Ken Norton in June, 1978. I lived in Easton, Pa. for about 8 months in early 1979, so it was about February, 1979 when I turned a corner in Easton, and passed him by. He was wearing a nice long overcoat.

12.   There was a bowling serendipity. I have always bowled with an average under 170 – usually about 160 or 165. A friend bowled in leagues and always carried an average in at least the high 170's. We went bowling together just once, I expecting to lose, and my games were higher: 202-222-202. I would love to take a lie detector test on that one, because my memory is quite clear on those scores. Nice round numbers.

13.I have been on some ongoing speaking terms with several sports announcers/journalists: P.J. Carlesimo, Rick Majerus, John Czarnecki, Navy roommate Bob Velin, and in one case the son of a very famous announcer (Chris Sheppard, son of Bob Sheppard, the "voice of God" at Yankee Stadium ballpark).

14.   There is at least one more serendipitous coincidence that is an extreme one that I could discuss confidentially, but not write about at this time.

"Papa, Trust Your Swing."

Qass Singh

www.ingramcontent.com/pod-product-compliance
Lightning Source LLC
Chambersburg PA
CBHW021839020426
42334CB00014B/703